EARLIER AMERICAN MUSIC
EDITED BY H. WILEY HITCHCOCK
for the *Music Library Association*

8

EDWARD MACDOWELL
PIANO PIECES

EDWARD MACDOWELL

PIANO PIECES
(Opp. 51, 55, 61, 62)

INTRODUCTION BY H. WILEY HITCHCOCK
Director, Institute for Studies in American Music,
Brooklyn College, CUNY

DA CAPO PRESS • NEW YORK • 1972

This Da Capo Press edition of Edward MacDowell's
Piano Pieces cumulates four collections of MacDowell's
piano music (Opp. 51, 55, 61, 62) published originally
between 1896 and 1902.

Library of Congress Catalog Card Number 70-170391
ISBN 0-306-77308-2

Copyright © 1972 by the Music Library Association

Published by Da Capo Press, Inc.
A Subsidiary of Plenum Publishing Corporation
227 West 17th Street, New York, New York 10011

EDITOR'S FOREWORD

American musical culture, from Colonial and Federal Era days on, has been reflected in an astonishing production of printed music of all kinds: by 1820, for instance, more than fifteen thousand musical publications had issued from American presses. Fads, fashions, and tastes have changed so rapidly in our history, however, that comparatively little earlier American music has remained in print. On the other hand, the past few decades have seen an explosion of interest in earlier American culture, including earlier American music. College and university courses in American civilization and American music have proliferated; recording companies have found a surprising response to earlier American composers and their music; a wave of interest in folk and popular music of past eras has opened up byways of musical experience unimagined only a short time ago.

It seems an opportune moment, therefore, to make available for study and enjoyment—and as an aid to furthering performance of earlier American music—works of significance that exist today only in a few scattered copies of publications long out of print, and works that may be well known only in later editions or arrangements having little relationship to the original compositions.

Earlier American Music is planned around several types of musical scores to be reprinted from early editions of the eighteenth, nineteenth, and early twentieth centuries. The categories are as follows:

> Songs and other solo vocal music
> Choral music and part-songs
> Solo keyboard music
> Chamber music
> Orchestral music and concertos
> Dance music and marches for band
> Theater music

The idea of *Earlier American Music* originated in a paper read before the Music Library Association in February, 1968, and published under the title "A Monumenta Americana?" in the Association's journal, *Notes* (September, 1968). It seems most appropriate, therefore, for the Music Library Association to sponsor this series. We hope *Earlier American Music* will stimulate further study and performance of musical Americana.

H. Wiley Hitchcock

INTRODUCTION

MacDowell published some sixteen collections of tone poems for piano. In this volume are reprinted the first editions of the last four. Aside from the Third and Fourth sonatas (1900 and 1901), these are his last and ripest piano compositions (*New England Idyls* and *Summer Wind* for women's chorus were, in fact, his last in any medium).

"Last and ripest" does not mean grandest and most pretentious. The sonatas, the *Virtuoso Studies* (Op. 46), of course the two piano concertos, and even some of the earlier character pieces attempt larger musical spans and are more demanding technically. Indeed, some individual pieces in these last four sets are so simple technically, so apparently artless, that for decades they have been given to fledgling pianists as "teaching pieces." We have thus tended to forget the essential shapeliness of each set, as we have tended to lose sight of the precision of craftsmanship in the separate compositions, and their remarkably instantaneous evocation of mood.

MacDowell may not have had the wide range of expression of the greatest masters of keyboard miniatures (François Couperin, the Debussy of *Préludes,* and Domenico Scarlatti come to mind), but his was a fully-formed, integrated, and identifiable style. He may thus be likened to Grieg (whose music he much admired) or Sibelius, who also purchased distinct individualities of style at the expense of range of expression.

MacDowell would not have been the "Romantic bard" that he was (the term is Gilbert Chase's) without mingling music and other arts. Not only, then, did he give suggestive titles to his pieces (and they reveal some favorite romantic themes — nature-love, nostalgia, exoticism, and mystery — within an American frame of reference); he often indited poems at the head of his musical portraits (as here in *Sea Pieces* and *New England Idyls*); and the evocative *fin-de-siècle* cover art of *Sea Pieces* is of his design. But such extra-musical props are not really essential to an admiration of the sharp etchings, the clearly incised cameos of the music itself.

H.W.H.

CONTENTS

Edward MacDowell
PIANO PIECES

Edition Schmidt.
... No. 47 ...

Woodland Sketches

... BY .

EDWARD MACDOWELL

Price, $1.25 net

Arthur P. Schmidt

BOSTON   LEIPZIG   NEW YORK
120 Boylston Street   8 West 40th Street

Elkin & Co., Ltd., London

I.

To a Wild Rose.

I.

To a Wild Rose.

Edward Mac Dowell.
Op. 51.

With simple tenderness. (♩ = 88 M.M.)

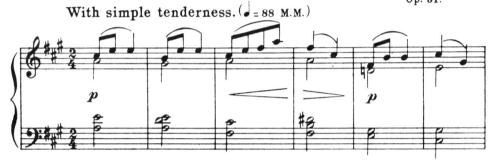

slightly marked

P.L.J. 403 a

II.
Will o' the Wisp.

II.

Will o' the Wisp.

EDWARD MAC DOWELL.
Op. 51.

Copyright.1896. by P. L. Jung.
Public Performance Permitted.
Assigned 1899 to Arthur P. Schmidt.

III.
At an old Trysting-place.

III.
At an old Trysting-place.

Edward Mac Dowell.

Op. 51.

Somewhat quaintly; not too sentimentally. ($\circ$ = 48)

P. L. J. 403 c

IV.

In Autumn.

IV.

In Autumn.

Edward Mac Dowell.
Op. 51.

Buoyantly, almost exuberantly. ($\bullet$ = 132)

P. L. J. 403 d

V.

From an Indian Lodge.

V.

From an Indian Lodge.

Edward Mac Dowell.
Op. 51.

Copyright, 1896, by P. L. Jung.
Public Performance Permitted. p

gradually retard.

Broadly.   *hold.*

p ⟨ ⟩   *ff* ⟨   *fff*

*) The upper notes of the octaves
    carry the melody   etc.

VI.
To a Water-lily.

VI.

To a Water-lily.

In dreamy, swaying rhythm. (♩ = 52)

EDWARD MAC DOWELL.
Op. 51.

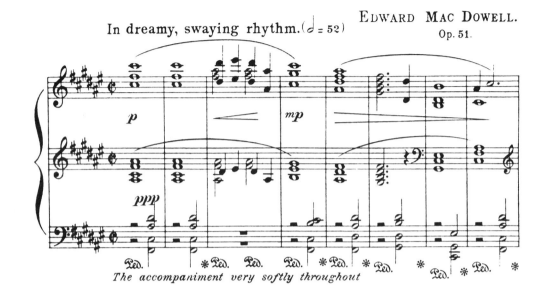

The accompaniment very softly throughout

with pedal

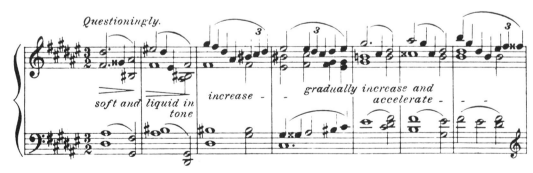

VII.

From Uncle Remus.

VII.

From Uncle Remus.

Edward Mac Dowell.
Op. 51.

With much humor; joyously.($\bullet$ = 126)

lightly

p

diminish, without dragging

VIII.

A Deserted Farm.

VIII.

A Deserted Farm.

Edward Mac Dowell.
Op. 51.

IX.
By a Meadow Brook.

IX.

By a Meadow Brook.

Edward Mac Dowell.
Op. 51.

Gracefully, merrily. ($\flat$ = 63)

Copyright, 1896, by P. L. Jung.
Public Performance Permitted.
Assigned 1899 to Arthur P. Schmidt.

X.

Told at Sunset.

X.

Told at Sunset.

EDWARD MAC DOWELL.
Op. 51.

Faster; sturdily. (♩ = 66)

SEA PIECES

Edward MacDowell

SEA PIECES

BY

Edward MacDowell.

Op. 55.

New York, P. L. Jung, Publisher

PRICE, $1.25 net.

I.

To the Sea.

"Ocean thou mighty monster."

To the Sea.

"Ocean, thou mighty monster."

Edward Mac Dowell.
Op. 55. No 1.

With dignity and breadth.

II.

From a Wandering Iceberg.

An errant princess of the north,
A virgin, snowy white
Sails adown the summer seas
To realms of burning light.

From a Wandering Iceberg.

An errant princess of the north,
A virgin, snowy white
Sails adown the summer seas
To realms of burning light.

EDWARD MAC DOWELL.
Op. 55, N?2.

Serenely. ♩ = 112.

As soft and smooth as possible.

P.L.J. 481 b

III.

A. D. MDCXX.

The yellow setting sun
  Melts the lazy sea to gold,
And gilds the swaying galleon
  That towards a land of promise
Lunges hugely on.

A. D. MDCXX.

The yellow setting sun
Melts the lazy sea to gold
And gilds the swaying galleon
That towards a land of promise
Lunges hugely on.

Edward Mac Dowell.
Op. 55, N° 3.

In unbroken rolling rhythm. ♩. = 58.

Sturdily and sternly, but without

change of rhythm.

IV.

Starlight.

The stars are but the cherubs
That sing about the throne
Of gray old Ocean's spouse,
Fair Moon's pale majesty.

Starlight.

The stars are but the cherubs
That sing about the throne
Of gray old Ocean's spouse,
Fair Moon's pale majesty.

EDWARD MAC DOWELL.
Op.55. N°4.

Tenderly. (♩ = 100.)

*) Chords marked ⌐ are not to be rolled.

P.L.J. 481 d

V.

Song.

A merry song, a chorus brave,
And yet a sigh regret
For roses sweet, in woodland lanes—
Ah, love can ne'er forget!

Song.

A merry song, a chorus brave,
And yet a sigh regret
For roses sweet, in woodland lanes—
Ah, love can ne'er forget!

Edward Mac Dowell.
Op. 55, No 5.

In changing moods.

VI.

From the Depths.

"And who shall sound the mystery of the sea?"

From the Depths.

"And who shall sound the mystery of the sea?"

EDWARD MAC DOWELL.
Op. 55. No 6.

In languid swaying rhythm.

with two pedals.

without soft pedal.

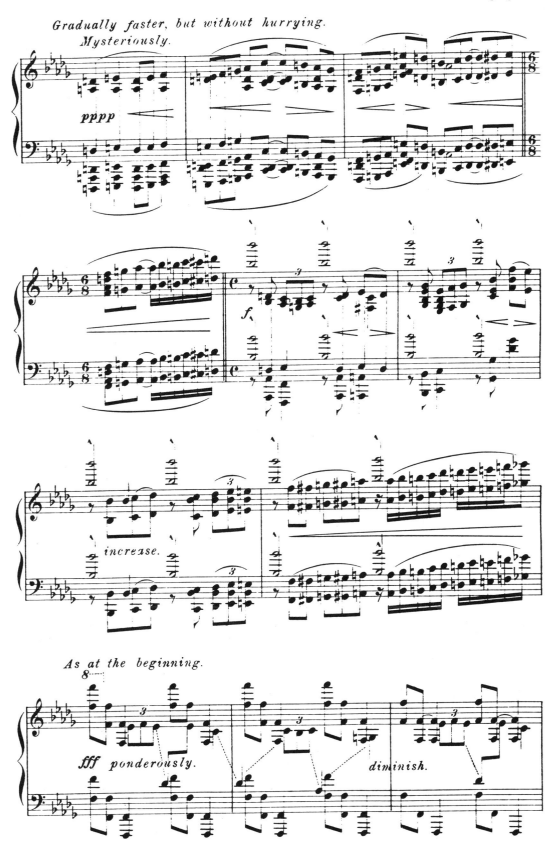

VII.

Nautilus.

"A fairy sail and a fairy boat."

Nautilus.

"A fairy sail and a fairy boat."

EDWARD MAC DOWELL.
Op. 55, No 7.

VIII.

In Mid-Ocean.

Inexorable!
  Thou straight line of eternal fate
That ring'st the world,
  Whil'st on thy moaning breast
We play our puny parts
  And reckon us immortal!

In Mid-Ocean.

Inexorable!
Thou straight line of eternal fate
That ring'st the world,
Whilst on thy moaning breast
We play our puny parts
And reckon us immortal!

EDWARD MAC DOWELL.
Op. 55, No 8.

gradually faster. - - - -

with sweep and power.

FIRESIDE TALES

composed for the pianoforte by

EDWARD MACDOWELL

no.1. An Old Love Story
no.2. Of Br'er Rabbit
no.3. From a German Forest
no.4. Of Salamanders
no.5. A Haunted House
no.6. By Smouldering Embers
Opus 61.
Price 1.25 Net.

The Arthur P. Schmidt Co.
Boston
120 Boylston St
New York
8 West 40th St

copyright 1902 by Arthur P. Schmidt

DESIGN BY G.C.PARKER · COPYRIGHT 1902 BY Arthur P. Schmidt

TO

Mrs. Seth Low.

AN OLD LOVE STORY.

EDWARD MAC DOWELL.
Op. 61. № 1.

A.P.S. 5772ª-19

OF BR'ER RABBIT.

EDWARD MAC DOWELL.
Op. 61. No 2.

FROM A GERMAN FOREST.

Edward Mac Dowell.
Op. 61. № 3.

OF SALAMANDERS.

EDWARD MAC DOWELL.
Op. 61. No. 4.

As delicately as possible. (♩. = about 50.)

With pedal

Copyright 1902 by Arthur P. Schmidt.
Public Performance Permitted.

A HAUNTED HOUSE.

Edward Mac Dowell.
Op. 61. № 5.

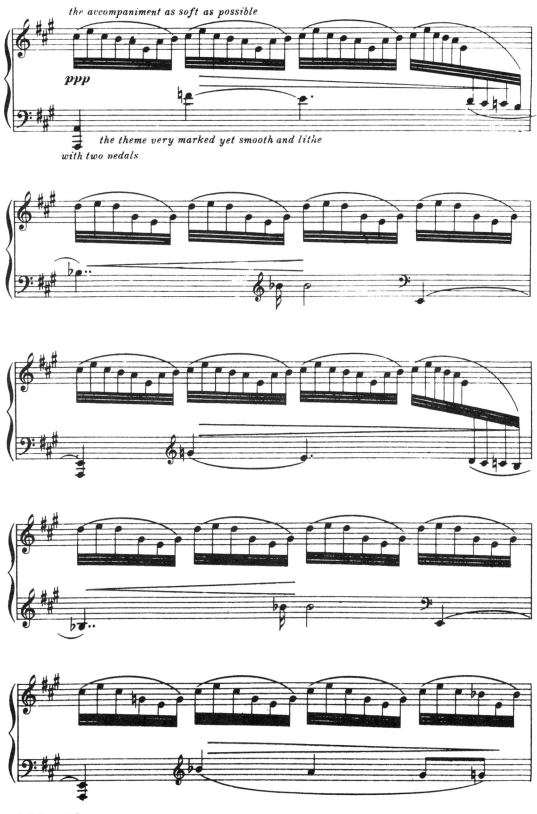

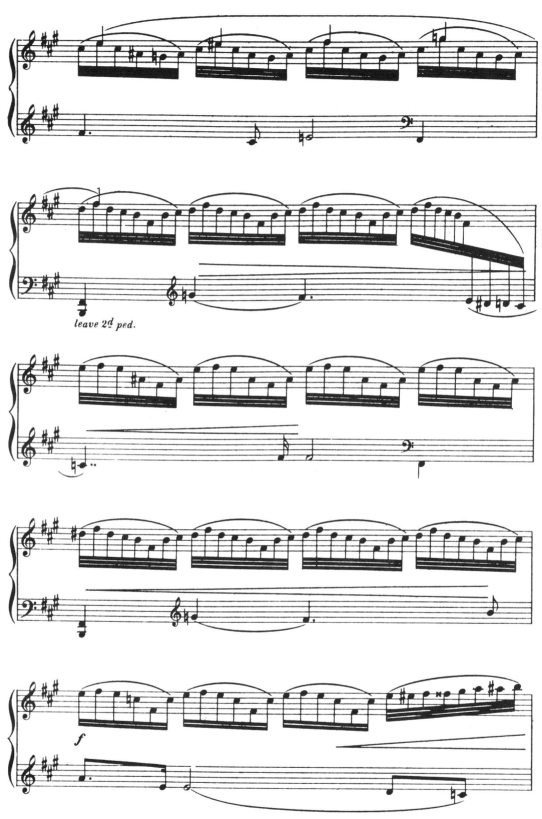

leave 2d ped.

f

BY SMOULDERING EMBERS.

Edward Mac Dowell.
Op. 61. No 6.

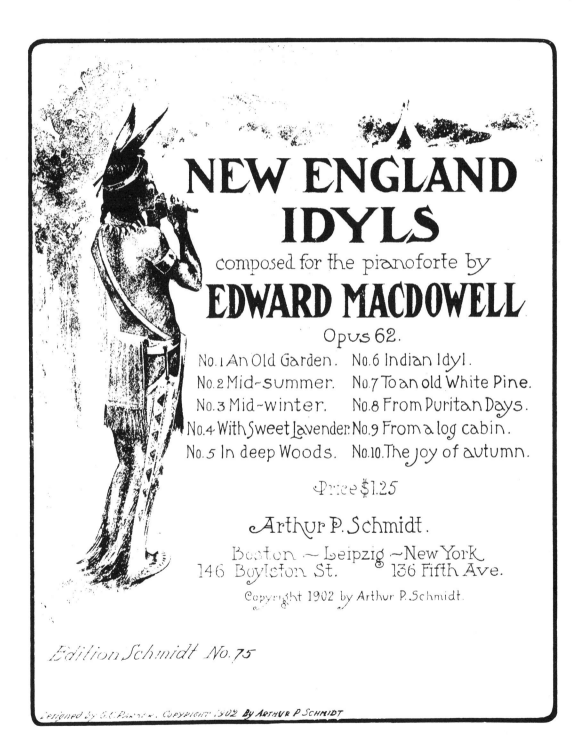

NEW ENGLAND IDYLS

composed for the pianoforte by

EDWARD MACDOWELL

Opus 62.

No.1 An Old Garden. No.6 Indian Idyl.
No.2 Mid-summer. No.7 To an old White Pine.
No.3 Mid-winter. No.8 From Puritan Days.
No.4 With Sweet Lavender. No.9 From a log cabin.
No.5 In deep Woods. No.10. The Joy of autumn.

Price $1.25

Arthur P. Schmidt.

Boston ~ Leipzig ~ New York
146 Boylston St. 136 Fifth Ave.

Copyright 1902 by Arthur P. Schmidt.

Edition Schmidt No. 75

I.

AN OLD GARDEN.

Sweet-alyssum,
　　Moss grown stair,
Rows of roses,
　　Larkspur fair.

All old posies,
　　Tokens rare
Of love undying
　　Linger there.

EDWARD MAC DOWELL.
Op. 62.

A.P.S. 5862ª-32

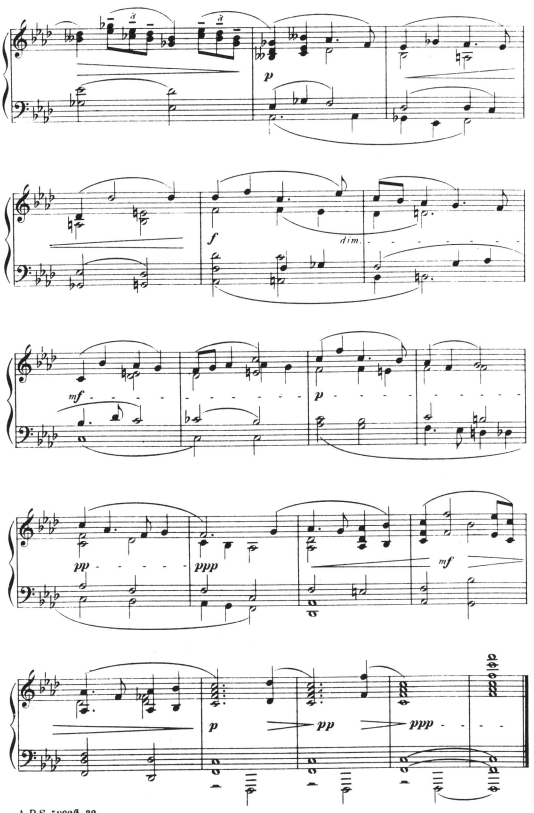

II.

MID-SUMMER.

Droning Summer slumbers on
Midst drowsy murmurs sweet.
Above, the lazy cloudlets drift,
Below, the swaying wheat.

EDWARD MAC DOWELL
Op. 62.

III.

MID-WINTER.

In shrouded awe the world is wrapped,
The sullen wind doth groan,
Neath winding-sheet the earth is stone,
The wraiths of snow have flown.

And lo! a thread of fate is snapped,
A breaking heart makes moan;
A virgin cold doth rule alone
From old Mid-winter's throne.

Edward Mac Dowell
Op. 62.

A.P.S. 58625-32

IV.

WITH SWEET LAVENDER.

From days of yore,
Of lover's lore,
A faded bow
Of one no more.

A treasured store
Of lover's lore,
Unmeasured woe
For one, no more.

EDWARD MAC DOWELL.
Op. 62.

With great tenderness and delicacy. (♩ = about 48.)

V.

IN DEEP WOODS.

Above, long slender shafts of opal flame,
Below, the dim cathedral aisles;
The silent mystery of immortal things
Broods o'er the woods at eve.

EDWARD MAC DOWELL.
Op. 62.

Broadly, impressively. (♩ = about 76.)

With pedal.

Copyright 1902 by Arthur P. Schmidt.
Public Performance Permitted.

mf with utmost volume of tone

very smooth,

pp

basses always very softly

yet emphatic

dim. - - -

ppp

pp

p

*) *Hold grace note d, with sust. pedal to the end.*

A.P.S. 58625-32

VI.

INDIAN IDYL.

Alone by the wayward flame
She weaves broad wampum skeins
While afar through the summer night
Sigh the wooing flutes' soft strains.

EDWARD MAC DOWELL.
Op. 62.

Copyright 1902 by Arthur P. Schmidt.
Public Performance Permitted.

VII.

TO AN OLD WHITE PINE.

A giant of an ancient race
He stands, a stubborn sentinel
O'er swaying, gentle forest trees
That whisper at his feet.

EDWARD MAC DOWELL.
Op. 62.

Gravely, with dignity. (♩ = about 84.)

VIII

FROM PURITAN DAYS.

"In Nomine Domini."

Edward Mac Dowell
Op. 62.

With measured emphasis. (♩ = about 54)

With pedal.

Copyright 1902 by Arthur P. Schmidt.
Public Performance Permitted.

IX.

FROM A LOG CABIN.

A house of dreams untold,
It looks out over the whispering tree-tops
And faces the setting sun.

EDWARD MAC DOWELL.
Op. 62.

With deep feeling. (♩ = about 48.)

X.

THE JOY OF AUTUMN.

From hill-top to vale,
Through meadow and dale,
Young Autumn doth wake the world
And naught shall avail,
But our souls shall sail
With the flag of life unfurled.

EDWARD MAC DOWELL.
Op. 62.

without retard.

F
FE